SALTLEY DEPOT

Andrew Cole

AMBERLEY

Acknowledgments

I would like to say a big thank you to some old Seagulls for helping me compile this book with their valuable insight and knowledge: Martin Wilkins, Cliff Webb and Phil Smith, many thanks.

First published 2018

Amberley Publishing
The Hill, Stroud
Gloucestershire, GL5 4EP

www.amberley-books.com

Copyright © Andrew Cole, 2018

The right of Andrew Cole to be identified as the Author of this work has been asserted in accordance with the Copyrights, Designs and Patents Act 1988.

ISBN 978 1 4456 8047 7 (print)
ISBN 978 1 4456 8048 4 (ebook)

British Library Cataloguing in Publication Data.
A catalogue record for this book is available from the British Library.

Origination by Amberley Publishing.
Printed in the UK.

Introduction

The original depot based at Saltley, Birmingham, was opened by the Midland Railway in 1854. The amount of traffic generated in the area meant that this depot was too small, and the lack of space meant it couldn't expand further. This meant that a new, bigger depot was built, where the current remnants of the depot are today on the main line from Birmingham to Derby, just outside of Birmingham city centre.

Originally, just the one roundhouse was built, but over time another two were added to the site, with the third being by far the largest of the three; this third roundhouse was built in 1900.

In 1935 the London, Midland & Scottish Railway recoded the shed as 21A. The Modernisation Plan of 1955 decided to do away with steam, and the shed was gradually run down and was closed to steam in 1967, but not before British Railways had recoded it as 2E.

In 1967 a new diesel fuel shed was built and the three roundhouses were demolished, with the coal stage also being demolished. The fuel shed consisted of three roads, and where the third roundhouse had stood, a new office and crew accommodation was built. Half of the land was sold off, and an industrial estate was built. Eventually, Saltley depot was given the shed code SY.

Being centrally placed, the train crews that were based at Saltley had very extensive route knowledge, and they were among some of the most respected and revered on the network. The name Saltley Seagulls was given to the crew, as they went everywhere, and also for other reasons!

Their sphere of operation spread from York in the north all the way down to Eastleigh in the south, and nearly everywhere in between.

Again, with its central location, almost any sort of traction could and has appeared on the depot, from the humble Class 08 right through to Class 92 electric locomotives, despite the fact that the depot isn't electrified.

Saltley depot was responsible for quite a few shunting locations, including Vauxhall carriage sidings, Washwood Heath, Bordseley, and also, unusually, Dorridge.

The depot was used to fuel and service both freight and passenger locomotives, finally coming under the control of Railfreight Distribution. In 1999 the depot passed to EWS.

The depot would see a downturn in traffic from this time onwards, as the Virgin Trains Class 47s were replaced with Class 220/221 units, resulting in the Class 47s no longer visiting. The new Class 66s meant that fewer of the older locomotives were needed, and also the yard at Washwood Heath being modernized, including a fuel line, meant that the depot shrunk in size. Another blow would be the loss of the Rover traffic from Longbridge, which towards the end was the main traffic for the depot; the loss of the Royal Mail contract was one of the final nails in the depot's coffin.

Saltley was to close in 2005, with the last loco, No. 47791, not leaving until 2008, but there is still a signing-on point for the remaining EWS staff based there. Today the fuel shed has been demolished, and all the rails lifted, with what is left being turned into a scrap yard – a very sad end to one of the more famous depots on British Rail.

No. 45067, 24 April 1966

LMS Black Five loco No. 45067 is seen stabled outside one of the three huge roundhouses. This was towards the end of this locomotive's working life and it would be withdrawn from Heaton Mersey shed in 1967, and was scrapped at Buttigiegs, Newport, in 1968.

No. 46490, 24 April 1966

No. 46490 is seen on the same day as the Black Five in the previous photograph, as part of a line of stabled steam locos. No. 46490 would be withdrawn from Newton Heath shed just over twelve months later, and was scrapped by Drapers of Hull in 1967.

No. 48133, 17 March 1967

LMS 8F locomotive No. 48133 is seen inside one of the roundhouses. The loco, like the roundhouse, had seen better days and No. 48133 was withdrawn from Royston shed in 1967, and would be scrapped by Drapers of Hull in February 1968.

D33, 21 May 1967

D33 (No. 45019) stands on one of the approach roads to the diesel shed while carrying plain green livery. Of note are the steam tender water-filler on the right, and also the houses on the left, which were later demolished to make way for the Freightliner terminal. D33 was renumbered 45019, and was scrapped by Vic Berry, Leicester, in 1986.

D46, 21 May 1967

D46 (No. 45037) stands in front of the coal stage while carrying plain green livery. Note the first generation DMU car to the right, and also the new diesel depot, which can be seen just above the Class 47s. D46 was later renumbered 45037 and was scrapped by M. C. Metals, Glasgow, in 1992.

D74, 21 May 1967

D74 (No. 45051) stands in front of the large No. 3 roundhouse. This roundhouse was added to the site in 1900, and was larger than the other two roundhouses. D74 was later renumbered 45051, and was scrapped by M. C. Metals, Glasgow, in 1989.

D86, 21 May 1967

D86 (No. 45105) is seen also stabled in front of the large No. 3 roundhouse. The roof of the roundhouse has all but gone in this view, and by this time, the shed had closed to steam. The little building to the left is the old weighbridge hut, as there was also a weighbridge situated at the depot. D86 would find a home in preservation at Barrow Hill, numbered 45105.

D1584, 21 May 1967

D1584 (Nos 47021, 47531, 47974, 47775) stands on one of the diesel depot approach roads carrying two-tone green livery, with small yellow ends. The white building in between the two locos is the, then new, signal box under construction. D1584 would undergo numerous renumberings, but would be scrapped in 2006 at Crewe diesel depot as No. 47775.

D1587, 21 May 1967

D1587 (No. 47464) is seen in the main stabling sidings in front of No. 3 roundhouse. This loco was renumbered 47464, and was a long-time Scottish-based loco, and it would be condemned following collision damage it received at Elgin when it hit No. 37416. It would be scrapped at Crewe Works in 1987.

D1765, 21 May 1967

D1765 (Nos 47170, 47582, 47733) rests inside the No. 3 roundhouse on one of its twenty-four roads. Unusually, a first generation DMU can be glimpsed outside the building, which looks ready to collapse. D1765 would eventually be renumbered 47733, and was scrapped by European Metal Recycling, Kingsbury, in 2008.

D5382, 21 May 1967

D5382 (No. 27034) stands inside one of the two smaller roundhouses while carrying two-tone green livery. Unusually, an MGR coal wagon can be seen on the adjacent road. D5382 was renumbered 27034, and was scrapped at Swindon Works in 1986.

D186, 28 May 1967

D186 (No. 46049) is seen inside the newly built diesel-fueling shed. This shed comprised three roads, and included inspection pits. D186 carries BR blue livery, and would be renumbered 46049, and was scrapped at Swindon Works in 1985.

D5382, 28 May 1967

D5382 (No. 27034) stands outside No. 3 roundhouse complete with brake tender. D5382 carries two-tone green livery – one that was only carried by this loco and D5380. D5382 was reallocated to Eastfield just two months later.

D1797, 30 July 1967

D1797 (No. 47316) is seen stabled carrying two-tone green livery. Of note is the impressive line up of 0-6-0 diesel shunters to the left, which were the old LMS Class 11 locomotives. The last of these shunters was withdrawn in 1971, with none gaining TOPS numbers. D1797 later became No. 47316.

D7655, 30 July 1967

D7655 (Nos 25305, 97251) stands in the main yard, along with a Class 45 Peak locomotive. The tall structure is the old mechanical ash-handling plant, which was used to speed up servicing steam locomotives. D7655 would eventually be renumbered as No. 97251 *Ethel 2* and was used in Scotland to provide steam heat to coaching stock.

D155, 6 August 1967

D155 (No. 46018) is seen outside No. 3 roundhouse carrying green livery with small yellow warning panels. This was later renumbered 46018. The Class 46s didn't survive as long as the Class 45 locomotives and No. 46018 was scrapped at Swindon Works in 1985.

D1701, 6 August 1967

D1701 (No. 47113) rests inside No. 3 roundhouse carrying two-tone green livery, but by this time it had received a full yellow front end. The loco is stabled underneath one of the huge supports for the roundhouse roof. D1701 was later renumbered 47113, and was scrapped by Vic Berry, Leicester, in 1990.

D1714, 6 August 1967

D1714 (No. 47124) stands in the yard next to the old steam coaling stage. This massive structure was used to load coal into the steam tenders, and it would be demolished in the summer of 1969. D1714 was later renumbered 47124, and was scrapped by M. C. Metals, Glasgow, in 1990.

D1875, 6 August 1967

D1875 (Nos 47356, 57001) stands on one of the roads inside No. 2 roundhouse, with the shot being taken from inside No. 3 roundhouse. The roads in the first two roundhouses were considerably shorter than the roads inside No. 3 roundhouse. D1875 would eventually be rebuilt as No. 57001.

D5657, 20 August 1967

D5657 (No. 31230) stands in the yard in front of the brick-built steam coal stage. These impressive structures used to be commonplace in the UK, but now only a couple survive, at Carnforth and Immingham. D5657 later became No. 31230.

D5190, 3 September 1967

D5190 (No. 25040) is seen outside the rapidly deteriorating No. 3 roundhouse. D5190 is seen coupled to a brake tender, which were common sights in the early days of BR diesels. D5190 was renumbered 25040 and would be scrapped at Swindon Works in 1982.

D68, 1 October 1967

D68 (No. 45046) carries BR blue livery, complete with full yellow ends, in the main stabling sidings. Of note are the large mechanical ash-handling plant above the cab and the recovery train to the left. D68 carries the name *Royal Fusilier*, and was scrapped carrying the number 45046 by M. C. Metals, Glasgow, in 1992.

D1822, 1 October 1967

D1822 (No. 47341) is seen stabled underneath the old coal stage. The new diesel fuel shed can be seen to the left, and the building in the background on the right is the No. 2 roundhouse. D1822 was later renumbered 47341, and was scrapped at Toton depot in 2003.

D1733, 22 October 1967

D1733 (Nos 47141, 47614, 47853) stands in front of No. 3 roundhouse. Although not obvious in this black and white photograph, D1733 carries XP64 blue livery, a precursor to BR blue. The large chimney in the background forms part of the sand house, and was used to dry out the sand before it was added to the locos.

D1517, 4 February 1968

D1517 (No. 47418) is seen outside No. 3 roundhouse carrying a 34G shed plate on the front. This was a Finsbury Park shed plate, although D1517 had been transferred to Tinsley by this time. D1517 was later renumbered 47418 and was scrapped at Frodingham in 1995.

No. 47163, 13 January 1980

No. 47163 (D1757, Nos 47610, 47823, 47787) is seen just twelve years after the previous shot, but all signs of the steam era shed have gone. The coal stage and mechanical ash-handling plant have been demolished, and the three roundhouses have also been demolished. No. 47163 stands on one of the departure roads, ready to leave the depot.

No. 25023, 4 April 1980

No. 25023 (D5173) stands on one of the departure roads. This was allocated to Haymarket, Edinburgh, at the time and only had five months' service life left, being withdrawn in September 1980 and scrapped at Swindon Works in 1983.

No. 47370, 31 January 1981

No. 47370 (D1889) stands where the old coal stage used to be sited and is carrying BR blue livery. This loco is fitted with an early form of multiple working equipment, which was only fitted to this loco and No. 47379 before it was removed.

No. 40195, 13 March 1982

No. 40195 (D395) sits on what became the outer siding of the depot. To the right-hand side, all of the tracks were lifted and a big industrial estate built over the railway land. No. 40195 would spend many years condemned at Crewe Works before finally being broken up in 1988.

No. 46037, 3 April 1982

No. 46037 (D174) is seen still retaining its domino-style headcode panel. This loco would carry this distinctive feature up until it was withdrawn. It was to suffer fire damage while working a passenger service at Kings Norton and was scrapped at Doncaster Works in 1985.

No. 55003, 14 September 1982

No. 55003 is seen moving onto one of the stabling sidings outside the main office block. It was unusual to see DMU cars on shed at Saltley, but these Class 122 cars were sometimes used as route learning cars. No. 55003 was happily preserved, and is today based on the Gloucestershire Warwickshire Railway.

No. 40129, 28 April 1983

No. 40129 (D329) moves off from the fueling shed, and is about to be stabled. Once the locos had been fuelled and inspected in the shed, just out of shot to the right, they would go down to the headshunt and then be positioned in the stabling sidings. No. 40129 was scrapped at Doncaster Works in 1984.

No. 46039, 8 September 1983

No. 46039 (D176) is seen stabled on a gloomy September day. This loco is stabled close to where the old coal stage used to be, with the diesel shed visible to the right. No. 46039 was scrapped at Swindon Works in 1985.

No. 47564, 17 April 1984

No. 47564 (D1619, Nos 47038, 47761) is seen near the end of the headshunt, having been refueled, and is preparing to stable to wait its next turn of duty. All the buildings in the background would eventually be demolished to make way for a car scrapyard.

No. 20088, 4 September 1984
No. 20088 (D8088, No. 2017) is seen having been refueled, and is making its way to the headshunt, along with classmate No. 20105. There used to be a line behind the Class 20s that was used to stable some of the many Class 08 locomotives that were allocated to Saltley, but by this time the line had been lifted.

No. 20105, 4 September 1984
No. 20105 (D8105, No. 2016) is seen on the same day as the previous photograph, and the Class 20s can be seen moving onto the stabling sidings. In the background on the left, the main line can be seen that links Birmingham New Street to Coventry and London Euston.

No. 20160, 18 September 1984

No. 20160 (D8160) stands on one of the stabling sidings, furthest away from the shed. These three lines would have been some of the approach roads to the No. 3 roundhouse, which was demolished to make way for the main office buildings.

No. 56108, 27 November 1984

No. 56108 stands outside the main office block while carrying large logo livery. The office block was built on the site of the old No. 3 roundhouse. No. 56108 would be scrapped by European Metal Recycling, Hartlepool, in 2011.

No. 56075, 8 February 1985

No. 56075 is seen in less than ideal weather conditions, while still carrying BR blue livery. The Class 25 to the right is No. 25027, which was stored in the same spot for nearly two years before being sent for scrap. No. 56075 was itself scrapped by Booth Roe Metals, Rotherham, in 2004.

No. 56080, 18 February 1985

No. 56080 is seen a week after the previous photograph, and the loco has been spruced up with red buffer beams and white trim around the bodyside grills and window surrounds. The white patch on the cabside is where the builder's plate has been removed.

No. 20195, 1 March 1985

No. 20195 (D8195) rests between duties along with another Class 20 and a couple of Class 58s. These locos were used on the coal traffic that originated from Daw Mill Colliery, and also coal workings to Didcot and Ironbridge.

No. 45146, 6 April 1985

No. 45146 (D66) is seen showing the changing face of freight locomotives at the time. The Class 25s and 45s were nearing the twilight of their careers; meanwhile, No. 58025, in between, was just starting out on its career. No. 45146 would be scrapped by M. C. Metals, Glasgow, in 1992.

No. 56066, 17 April 1985

No. 56066 is seen on the middle of the three stabling sidings in front of the main office block. Both outer lines would become redundant by 1987 and would be lifted, leaving just the line that No. 56066 stands on in situ. The signal box, across the main Birmingham to Derby line, can be seen in the left background behind the Class 47.

No. 40122, 30 April 1985

No. 40122 (D200) stands in BR green livery, awaiting its next turn of duty. Saltley, with its central location, always seemed to play host to some of the more exotic motive power to be found, and you never knew what was going to turn up next. No. 40122 was preserved at the National Railway Museum, York.

No. 73106, 23 May 1985

No. 73106 (E6012) is seen just three weeks after the previous photograph, and just goes to emphasize the point of strange oddities turning up at Saltley. Class 73s were never an everyday sight at the depot, and indeed their appearances can be counted on one hand.

No. 33034, 25 May 1985

No. 33034 (D6552) is seen stabled alongside a Class 56 and a Class 58. Saltley men were trained up on Class 33s for a tank train that was to run to Eastleigh, but the turn never materialised. No. 33034 would eventually be preserved at the Swanage Railway, but was broken up for spares in 2013.

No. 47575, 29 June 1985

No. 47575 (D1770, No. 47175) is seen on one of the departure roads, awaiting its next turn of duty. This had been named *City of Hereford* just three days earlier as part of the GWR 150th anniversary celebrations. It had been renumbered from 47175 when it was fitted with ETH equipment and was finally scrapped by C. F. Booth, Rotherham, in 2010.

No. 45143, 29 September 1985

No. 45143 (D62) is seen coming back from the headshunt having been refueled, and is about to be stabled, awaiting its next turn of duty. This carries the name *5th Royal Inniskilling Dragoon Guards 1685–1985*, and the date had only recently been applied. No. 45143 was eventually broken up for scrap by M. C. Metals, Glasgow, in 1994.

No. 142009, 26 October 1985

No. 142009 is seen stabled on the line that leads round the back of the fuel shed. This was a highly unusual visitor to Saltley, possibly being the only Class 142 to visit the depot, and it carries GMPTE orange and brown livery. Class 142s have never been allocated around Birmingham, and No. 142009 is still in service today with Northern.

No. 20049, 26 December 1985

No. 20049 (D8049) spends Christmas 1985 stabled at Saltley, along with white stripe carrying No. 31411. The two days around Christmas were the only two days where you were more or less guaranteed access to the depot, as there were no loco movements planned.

No. 47634, 4 January 1986

No. 47634 (D1751, No. 47158) *Henry Ford* is seen on one of the departure roads. This had only just been refurbished and renumbered from 47158, and it would go on to spend many months stored at Saltley awaiting disposal, which was completed by European Metal Recycling, Kingsbury, in 2004.

No. 25199, 11 January 1986

No. 25199 (D7549) is seen stabled on one of the roads that would soon be taken out of use. Class 25s were very common visitors to Saltley, with nearby Bescot and also Crewe having sizeable allocations. No. 25199 would be scrapped by Vic Berry, Leicester, in 1989.

No. 20059, 8 February 1986

No. 20059 (D8059, No. 20302) is seen stabled in the winter sunshine after a sprinkling of snow. Class 20 locomotives were also very common visitors to Saltley, and No. 20059 is seen having recently been repainted into red stripe Railfreight livery. This loco would carry the number 20302 for a short while before reverting back to 20059, and it was happily preserved.

No. 47363, 8 February 1986

No. 47363 (D1882) is seen on the same day as the previous photograph, and shows No. 47363 carrying the name *Billingham Enterprise*, and also a Thornaby Kingfisher symbol. The Thornaby Class 47s were used on steel and oil workings, and were always good to see with their local North East embellishments.

No. 47379, 15 March 1986

No. 47379 (D1898) is seen awaiting departure from Saltley. This loco had recently gained Railfreight livery, and the red stripe version had yet to be applied, despite the Class 58 in the background carrying it. No. 47379 was named *Total Energy* just a couple of weeks later, and it would be scrapped by EWS at Wigan Springs Branch in 2000.

No. 47459, 29 March 1986

No. 47459 (D1579) is seen stabled carrying large logo livery. Just past the blue Class 47, on the adjacent line to the right, is where the coal stage used to be situated, with the diesel refueling shed to the right behind the Class 31. No. 47459 would be scrapped by Booths, Rotherham, in 1993.

No. 56066, 3 May 1986

No. 56066 is seen carrying original Railfreight livery while stabled awaiting its next turn. Class 56s were used on coal traffic in the area, with regular workings down to Didcot and Ironbridge. This loco would suffer collision damage and received a cab from withdrawn classmate No. 56122, and was eventually scrapped by Ron Hull Junior, Rotherham, in 2005.

No. 47492, 2 June 1986

No. 47492 (D1760) is seen, along with a great mix of other traction, while carrying InterCity Scotrail livery. Also in the view are another three BR blue Class 47s, a Class 45 Peak, and also two Class 50 locomotives, including No. 50007 carrying GWR green livery. Just out of shot to the right was Deltic No. 55015 *Tulyar*.

No. 55015, 2 June 1986

No. 55015 (D9015) *Tulyar* is seen, somewhat strangely, stabled on one of the fuel depot entry roads. This was at the time when Deltic locomotives were to be seen at various open days across the network, and No. 55015 was visiting Saltley after appearing at one open day and while making its way to the next.

No. 50023, 21 June 1986

No. 50023 (D423) *Howe* is seen waiting to depart the depot. This had only just received a coat of Network SouthEast livery, which certainly stood out on these locomotives. Class 50s were also regular visitors around this time, with workings down to Poole and Bristol from Birmingham New Street, and you could almost guarantee a couple to be on shed of a weekend.

No. 56103, 19 July 1986

No. 56103 is seen stabled outside the main office block, carrying large logo livery. The offices were built on the site of the large No. 3 roundhouse, and the white wall just visible behind the far cab of No. 56103 is part of one of the two smaller roundhouses, which was all that remained of the mighty structure at this time.

No. 37294, 19 August 1986

No. 37294 (D6994) is seen carrying BR blue livery, awaiting its next turn of duty. This loco was in fact acting as the Lickey bank loco this day, along with classmate No. 37244, which it is coupled with. This was regularly rostered as a pair of Cardiff-allocated Class 37s, but they rarely ventured up to Saltley, normally staying near Bromsgrove. The Lickey Incline still requires a bank engine to this day, although it is now a DB Cargo Class 66.

No. 37304, 23 August 1986

No. 37304 (D6604, Nos 37272, 37334) is seen stabled in front of the office block, carrying BR blue livery. The industrial estate behind was built on part of the No. 3 roundhouse, which was demolished in the late 1960s. No. 37304 was allocated to Cardiff Canton at the time, and the Class 37/3 locomotives were very rarely seen this far north.

No. 50035, 8 September 1986

No. 50035 (D435, 50135) is seen stabled at a very quiet Saltley while carrying Network SouthEast livery. This would soon depart back towards London Paddington, and of note is the large crest situated underneath the *Ark Royal* nameplate. No. 50035 would be preserved and is today based at the Severn Valley Railway.

No. 140001, 9 September 1986

No. 140001 is seen passing Saltley with what appears to be an empty stock working, as there are no passengers aboard. Although not taken on the depot, I have included this shot to show that almost anything could be seen around Saltley. No. 140001 was happily preserved at the Keith & Dufftown Railway in Scotland.

No. 50044, 26 December 1986

No. 50044 (D444) *Exeter* is seen stabled on one of the departure roads. This was taken on Boxing Day 1986; there were always a large number of locomotives stabled on the depot as the network shut down for the Christmas period.

No. 31450, 6 April 1987

No. 31450 (D5551, No. 31133) is seen stabled along with Class 56 No. 56066. This was one of the ETH-fitted Class 31s that were used on passenger workings and it is also one of the skinhead Class 31/4s, of which there were only four, Nos 31418, 31444 and 31461 being the other three.

No. 45127, 9 April 1987

No. 45127 (D87) is seen nearing the end of its working life at a very sparse Saltley. This would only have one more month left in service, and would spend many months in storage at March before finally being scrapped by a private contractor at Crewe in 1994.

No. 20084, 10 April 1987

No. 20084 (D8084, No. 20302) is seen, unusually, stabled as just a single Class 20 in front of the fuel shed. This had been modified with larger fuel tanks, which can be seen in front of the cab with the BR double arrow on. No. 20084 would go on to be rebuilt by DRS and was renumbered 20302.

No. 37149, 11 April 1987

No. 37149 (D6849, No. 37892) is seen having been rerailed following a derailment while stabling. This was unfortunately a common occurrence at Saltley, with the track work not being the best. The BRUFF rerailing truck was based at Tyseley, so it was not far for it to come and help out. No. 37149 was rebuilt as No. 37892 in the Class 37 refurbishment programme.

No. 47350, 25 April 1987

No. 47350 (D1831, No. 57005) is seen having been spruced up for its naming ceremony. It would be named *British Petroleum* three days later. No. 47350 would eventually be rebuilt as No. 57005.

No. 31309, 1 June 1987

No. 31309 (D5843) *Cricklewood* is seen banking a heavy steel working past the depot. This was a regular duty for Saltley men, having originally been in the hands of Class 25 locomotives. The bank pilot would stable down by Saltley viaduct awaiting its next working, and would bank freights up past Bordesley towards Moseley on the Camp Hill line.

No. 47572, 13 June 1987

No. 47572 (D1763, No. 47168) is seen stabled outside the main depot buildings, carrying large logo livery and the name *Ely Cathedral*. Being based at Stratford, East London, this would probably have arrived on a service from Norwich or Great Yarmouth.

No. 45107, 22 June 1987

No. 45107 (D43) is seen stabling in the yard after being refuelled. As can be seen in the background, by this time all the factories and buildings had been demolished, and the site would eventually house a scrapyard, which it still does to this day. No. 45107 carries the unofficial Tinsley name of *Phoenix*.

No. 58045, 5 July 1987

No. 58045 stands outside the main office block carrying red stripe Railfreight livery. By this time, the line in the foreground had been taken out of use and it would eventually be lifted, along with the line behind the Class 58, leaving just the one stabling siding at this part of the depot.

No. 47618, 3 October 1987

No. 47618 (D1609, Nos 47030, 47836, 47780) is seen acting as a depot shunter while carrying InterCity livery. No. 47618 carries the name *Fair Rosamund*, and would carry various running numbers over the years, before finally becoming No. 47780. It was scrapped by European Metal Recycling, Kingsbury, in 2007.

No. 47484, 9 October 1987

No. 47484 (D1662) is seen stabled along with classmate No. 47628. Both locomotives carry GWR green livery, and both were based on the Western Region at the time. There were originally four Class 47s painted in this livery, but by this time only three remained. No. 47484 carries the name *Isambard Kingdom Brunel*, and No. 47628 carries the name *Sir Daniel Gooch*.

No. 37200, 26 December 1987

No. 37200 (D6900, No. 37377) is seen spending Christmas 1987 on one of the departure roads, carrying red stripe Railfreight livery. The fuel shed can be seen to the right, and the office block to the left, with the main line behind the photographer. No. 37200 was renumbered 37377, and was scrapped by C. F. Booth, Rotherham, in 2009.

No. 45140, 26 December 1987

No. 45140 (D102) is seen at a busy depot on Boxing Day 1987. This was one of the few times you were given permission to get photos on the depot, with there being no booked movements during the two-day Christmas shut-down. No. 45140 is another Class 45 to carry an unofficial name, this being *Mercury*.

No. 47079, 26 December 1987

No. 47079 (D1664, No. 57009) is seen on one of the departure roads, carrying Trainload Construction livery. This livery had only been launched in October of that year and No. 47079 was formerly painted in GWR green livery, which matched Nos 47484 and 47628 from a couple of photographs previous.

No. 47583, 18 May 1988

No. 47583 (D1767, Nos 47172, 47734) *County of Hertfordshire* stands outside the fuel shed carrying original Network SouthEast livery. The line behind the Class 47 was a headshunt and No. 47583 is stabled roughly underneath where the coal stage would have been situated. No. 47583 was eventually renumbered 47734 in the RES fleet.

No. 47656, 19 June 1988

No. 47656 (D1719, Nos 47128, 47811) is seen carrying large logo livery. The last batch of ETH-fitted Class 47s had only been completed in 1986, with No. 47656 being renumbered from 47128. It would go on to be renumbered 47811 when it was fitted with larger fuel tanks.

No. 47283, 12 July 1988

No. 47283 (D1985) is seen returning from the headshunt to be stabled on one of the stabling roads. This loco is seen carrying Trainload Speedlink livery, and this scheme quickly replaced BR blue on a large number of Class 47s. These locos were used on trip workings that originated in the area, mainly from Washwood Heath Yard.

No. 47636, 17 November 1988

No. 47636 (D1920, Nos 47243, 47777) *Sir John de Graeme* is seen stabled carrying large logo livery. This loco was based at Eastfield depot at the time and Scottish-based Class 47 locomotives were quite common visitors to Saltley, normally arriving on passenger turns from Edinburgh.

No. 47341, 23 November 1988

No. 47341 (D1822) is seen carrying large logo livery. This was the only member of the Class 47/3 locomotives to carry this livery. As can be seen in the background, a start had been made on using the former factory site as a scrapyard, with the Dunn Brothers equipment in situ.

No. 20088, 4 February 1989

No. 20088 (D8088, No. 2017) is seen on the departure roads carrying unbranded Trainload Freight livery. This was the only Class 20 in BR service to carry this livery, although a few more have carried it in preservation. This shot was taken from the staff car park, and the fuel shed would be situated behind the Class 58 to the left.

No. 47347, 12 May 1989

No. 47347 (D1828, No. 57004) stands on one of the stabling sidings carrying Trainload Metals livery and also a Thornaby Kingfisher. Thornaby locos were again common visitors to Saltley, normally arriving on steel traffic. Thornaby always used to take great pride in their locos, often giving them local embellishments. No. 47347 was rebuilt as No. 57004.

No. 47825, 12 May 1989

No. 47825 (D1759, Nos 47165, 47590, 57601) is seen stabled carrying InterCity Mainline livery and also the name *Thomas Telford*. The large signal box can be seen behind the Class 47; it would close in November 2016, with control passing to the nearby West Midlands Signaling Centre.

No. 4498, 18 July 1989

No. 4498 (60007) *Sir Nigel Gresley* is seen stabled outside the main fuel shed along with its support coach. Since the end of British Rail steam operations in 1968, visits of preserved steam locos to Saltley have been very rare, although a large number of railtours have passed by the depot.

No. 47705, 22 July 1989

No. 47705 (D1957, 47554, 57303) is seen carrying Network SouthEast livery, having just transferred to the Western Region from the Scottish Region. This used to carry the name *Lothian* when it was based in Scotland, and this was the day my brother copped his last Class 47!

No. 47227, 27 July 1989

No. 47227 (D1903) is seen stabled at the end of the dead-end road while carrying red stripe Railfreight livery. The rake of TTA diesel fuel tanks can be seen in the background; they were normally tripped to the depot from Washwood Heath yard. No. 47227 was scrapped by Coopers Metals, Attercliffe, in 1994.

No. 47834, 6 August 1989

No. 47834 (D1656, Nos 47072, 47609, 47798) *Fire Fly* is seen stabled, having been recently repainted into InterCity Swallow livery. This loco was to be used on Royal Train workings, along with No. 47835; both were eventually renumbered into the Class 47/7 series, with No. 47834 becoming No. 47798. It is today part of the National Collection, based in York.

No. 31105, 8 August 1989

No. 31105 (D5523) is seen banking an MGR working past Saltley while carrying red stripe Railfreight livery. The coal traffic in the Midlands used to originate from Daw Mill Colliery, and from time to time from Three Spires, and it would head for Ironbridge and Didcot power stations.

No. 58004, 25 September 1989

No. 58004 is seen stabled, carrying Trainload Coal livery. The Class 58s were used on coal traffic in the Midlands. As can be seen, the line in the foreground had been lifted by this time. No. 58004 is currently stored out of use in Alizay, northern France.

No. 31102, 30 September 1989

No. 31102 (D5520) carries original Railfreight livery while stabled along with Class 47 No. 47509. The Class 31s were often used on local trip workings in the area, and were also put to work on ballast jobs. In previous times, they were also used on passenger workings through to Leicester and Norwich, and occasionally up towards Sheffield.

No. 47146, 9 December 1989

No. 47146 (D1739) is seen near the end of the headshunt, having been rerailed using the Tyseley-based BRUFF rerailing van. The track work around the depot never looked in the best of shape, and the rerailing gang was used quite often at the depot.

No. 31400, 26 December 1989

No. 31400 (D5579, 31161) is seen at a busy depot during Christmas 1989. No. 31400 was refurbished from No. 31161 to act as a replacement for one of the two withdrawn ETH Class 31/4s, for use on passenger workings in the North West. Nos 31436 and 31443 were withdrawn early, with Nos 31400 and 31469 being their replacements. No. 31400 would itself be scrapped by C. F. Booth, Rotherham, in 1993.

No. 37258, 6 July 1990

No. 37258 (D6958, No. 37384) is seen stabled, carrying departmental grey livery. This is roughly where the coal stage used to be situated, and No. 37258 would go on to be renumbered 37384. Despite there being three Class 37s in this view, they were never as common a visitor to Saltley as the Class 47s.

No. 37054, 8 July 1990

No. 37054 (D6754) is seen carrying recently applied departmental grey livery. This livery was very dull and it would be relieved by a yellow stripe along the top of the loco. No. 37054 would eventually be broken up by a private contractor at Motherwell depot in 2003.

No. 37906, 8 July 1990

No. 37906 (D6906, No. 37206) is seen stabled outside the fuel shed. This is another shot taken from the staff car park, with the main line from Birmingham to Derby on the right. No. 37906 carries Trainload Metals livery, and can today be found at Leicester depot.

No. 58007, 8 July 1990

No. 58007 is seen carrying Trainload Coal livery. As can be seen, by this time the scrapyard in the background had grown, and a large framework had to be erected so that the scrap vehicles didn't fall onto the running lines! No. 58007 is another Class 58 that is today stored at Alizay in northern France.

No. 37510, 29 July 1990

No. 37510 (D6812, No. 37112) is seen arriving at the depot carrying Trainload Metals livery. This was the only access point to the depot, with the Class 47 in the background standing on the main lines. The fuel shed is located behind and to the left, which is where the Class 37 is heading.

No. 47375, 29 July 1990

No. 47375 (D1894, No. 047375) is seen running onto the depot carrying Trainload Speedlink livery. No. 47375 also carries the name *Tinsley Traction Depot*, and it was involved in moving steam loco No. 5080 *Defiant* on this day. No. 47375 has since left the UK for a new career in Hungary.

No. 47633, 23 September 1990

No. 47633 (D1668, No. 47083) is seen stabled among other Class 47s and a Class 37. No. 47633 carries an Eastfield Scottie Dog logo, and would only have two more months' service life left, being withdrawn in the November. No. 47633 was converted from one of the original Western Region named Class 47s, No. 47083 *Orion*, and it was scrapped by M. C. Metals, Glasgow, in 1994.

No. 47706, 25 January 1991

No. 47706 (D1936, No. 47494) is seen carrying ScotRail livery while stabled. By this time, ScotRail had finished using the Class 47/7s, and the majority had transferred south, either to Network SouthEast or to the Parcels sector, for which No. 47706 was used. It would be scrapped at Crewe Works in 1995.

No. 31312, 23 February 1991

No. 31312 (D5846) stands outside the depot while on bank pilot duty. This loco carries Trainload Coal livery, and is complete with a set of miniature snowploughs attached. The bank pilot was still retained at this time, until the more powerful Class 60 locomotives started to appear, which resulted in the need for the bank engine to be reduced.

No. 58043, 24 February 1991

No. 58043 (L37) stands outside the main office block while carrying Trainload Coal livery. Note the water tank on top of the building to the right. Today all of the buildings have been swept away, and all the lines have been lifted, leaving nothing of this once huge depot.

No. 56110, 8 April 1991

No. 56110 is seen stabled, carrying Trainload Construction livery. The Construction Class 56s were used on workings out of Mountsorrel in Leicestershire, and also from Croft on the Leicester to Nuneaton line. This siding always seemed to be home to the Class 58s and 56s.

No. 47475, 14 April 1991

No. 47475 (D1603) is seen carrying its unique TransPennine livery. This was the only class member to carry this livery, and by this time it had been transferred to the Parcels sector, who were never the quickest to repaint their locomotives. No. 47475 would be scrapped by T. J. Thompson, Stockton, in 2008.

No. 158781, 14 April 1991

No. 158781 is seen stabled on the dead-end road along with classmate No. 158755. It was highly unusual to get diesel units stabled on the depot, but when the Class 158s were introduced, they did appear from time to time. No. 158781 has since been renumbered 158887, and works for South Western Railway.

No. 47309, 19 April 1991

No. 47309 (D1790, No. 47389) *The Halewood Transmission* is seen carrying Trainload Speedlink livery. The Class 47 was the staple motive power by this time and they would be used on almost any sort of working, and they were heavily used on automotive traffic from the Rover factory at Longbridge.

No. 47555, 6 June 1991

No. 47555 (D1717, No. 47126) is seen carrying original InterCity livery, along with classmate No. 47471. The IC Class 47s were used on passenger workings, mainly towards Bristol, but also towards the North East. No. 47555 carries the name *The Commonwealth Spirit* and would eventually pass to Railfreight Distribution.

No. 37431, 23 June 1991

No. 37431 (D6972, No. 37272) is seen waiting to depart from the depot on one of the departure roads. No. 37431 was the final Class 37/4 converted and was one of the first to be withdrawn. It carries the name *Bullidae*, and also small Trainload Petroleum logos on the cabside. No. 37431 was scrapped at Wigan Springs Branch in 2000.

No. 47125, 9 September 1991

No. 47125 (D1715) is seen carrying Trainload Petroleum livery. This was one of the Crewe-allocated Class 47s that were outbased at Stanlow for petroleum traffic, and the scar on the bodyside is where the name *Tonnidae* has been removed.

No. 08765, 10 November 1991

No. 08765 (D3933) is seen coupled to a rake of TTA diesel fuel tanks. This short line was where the tanks were kept until they were tripped back to Washwood Heath. Saltley used to be responsible for shunting locomotives at various places, including Bordseley, Kings Norton, Vauxhall, Washwood Heath Main Yard, Washwood Heath West Yard and also Dorridge.

No. 08928, 26 December 1991

No. 08928 (D4158) is seen stabled outside the fuel shed along with classmate No. 08893. These were long-time Saltley-allocated Class 08s, with No. 08928 eventually departing for Norwich, where the red stripe was replaced with a blue stripe.

No. 31324, 26 December 1991

No. 31324 (D5859) takes a break from bank pilot duty as it spends Christmas 1991 stabled on the fuel tank road. At this time, the bank engine was normally a Crewe-based Trainload Coal Class 31, and No. 31324 looks good with a set of miniature snowploughs attached.

No. 47281, 26 December 1991

No. 47281 (D1983) is seen carrying Trainload Speedlink livery on a very quiet Boxing Day 1991. This is roughly where the coal stage used to be situated, hence the large space between the sidings. In the early days, the depot and yard used to extend behind the locos, and the industrial estate has been built on the former sidings.

No. 47809, 26 December 1991

No. 47809 (D1640, Nos 47056, 47654, 47783) *Finsbury Park* is seen stabled, waiting on one of the departure roads. The large power signal box can be seen behind, which was separated from the depot by the Birmingham to Derby main line. No. 47809 would be renumbered 47783 when it was transferred to RES.

No. 153307, 8 March 1992

No. 153307 is seen stabled outside the fuel shed having just been rebuilt from a Class 155 car, with the addition of a new cab, which can be seen in this shot. This could possibly have been visiting the depot for crew training, and it is still in use today with Northern, based at Neville Hill.

No. 56014, 22 March 1992

No. 56014 is seen stabled, carrying Trainload Coal livery. By this time, the Class 56s were becoming less common visitors to the Midlands, following the introduction of the Class 60s on coal traffic, with the Class 56s being used more in Yorkshire and the North East. No. 56014 would be scrapped at Immingham in 2000.

No. 47845, 31 May 1992

No. 47845 (D1653, Nos 47069, 47638, 57301) *County of Kent* is seen waiting its turn in the queue for the fuel pumps. This shot has been taken from the opposite side of the main line, next to the power signal box. All is not well with No. 47845 judging by the large oil stain on the bodyside.

No. 47521, 15 July 1992

No. 47521 (D1104) is seen stabled while carrying Network SouthEast livery. With largescale withdrawals of the Class 50s having taken place, the Class 47s took over many of their workings, although by this time the Class 47s would soon be replaced and transferred to parcels traffic. No. 47521 would be withdrawn with collision damage, and was scrapped at Crewe Works in 1995.

No. 47573, 26 July 1992

No. 47573 (D1768, Nos 47173, 47762) is seen stabled on one of the departure roads, carrying Rail Express Systems livery. This loco was famous as being one of the first Class 47s to receive Network SouthEast livery, but by this time had transferred to parcels use.

No. 60087, 26 July 1992

No. 60087 *Siloch* is seen stabled next to the office block, carrying Trainload Coal livery. The coal examples were the most numerous to be seen on the depot, but Class 60s from all sectors used to pass regularly. The first Class 60 to appear on Saltley was No. 60008 in 1990, for crew training.

No. 60088, 14 September 1992

No. 60088 is seen when still relatively new carrying Trainload Coal livery. There were some very hard to pronounce names applied to the Class 60s, including the *Buachaille Etive Mor* plate fitted to No. 60088.

No. 47704, 21 March 1993

No. 47704 (D1937, No. 47495) appears to be the only loco stabled on the shed on this particular day. No. 47704 was transferred straight from ScotRail to the parcels sector in 1990, and would eventually be scrapped in 2006 by Ron Hull Junior, Rotherham.

No. 60083, 21 March 1993

No. 60083 *Shining Tor* is seen stabled carrying Trainload Construction livery. This was outbased at Leicester at the time for aggregate workings out of Mountsorrel, and has a Leicester Tiger depot sticker just underneath the coupling.

No. 37426, 2 April 1993

No. 37426 (D6999, No. 37299) is seen carrying InterCity Mainline livery while stabled on the dead-end road. This loco had been rebuilt from No. 37299 for passenger workings out of Cardiff, and would eventually be repainted into EWS maroon livery. No. 37426 was scrapped by C. F. Booth, Rotherham, in 2013.

No. 37162, 11 April 1993

No. 37162 (D6862) is seen a week after the previous photograph, along with No. 37426, which was still working off Saltley. No. 37162 carries departmental grey livery, but has had small Trainload Petroleum logos applied. This loco would be scrapped by Booth Roe Metals, Rotherham, in 2005.

No. 47369, 27 June 1993

No. 47369 (D1888) is seen stabled among other Class 47s, with each carrying a different livery. Class 47s were the most common visitor to Saltley at this time, until the arrival of the Class 66s started to eliminate them from the network. No. 47369 carries Trainload Petroleum livery.

No. 47833, 3 July 1993

No. 47833 (D1962, Nos 47262, 47608, 47788) is seen carrying a unique version of the old British Rail two-tone green livery. This had been repainted by InterCity, and the loco also received the name *Captain Peter Manisty RN*. It was later renumbered 47788.

No. 60032, 31 July 1993

No. 60032 *William Booth* is seen outside the main office block carrying Trainload Coal livery. This was one of just a handful of the class to receive plaques from new above the nameplates. William Booth was the founder of the Salvation Army.

No. 47596, 1 August 1993

No. 47596 (D1933, 47255) *Aldeburgh Festival* is seen carrying Network SouthEast livery. By this time, NSE had finished using the Class 47s, and most had transferred to the parcels sector, including No. 47596. Today this loco can be found at the Mid-Norfolk Railway, still carrying its NSE livery.

No. 20075, 11 August 1993

No. 20075 (D8075, 20309) is seen stabled along with classmate No. 20131 on the dead-end road. Both of these locos had not long been through Doncaster Works for refurbishment, and they were to find use with British Rail Telecommunications on signaling trains. They would both eventually be sold to Direct Rail Services.

No. 08413, 26 December 1993

No. 08413 (D3528) is seen coupled to the TTA diesel fuel tanks over Christmas 1993. This Class 08 had not long transferred from Stratford depot, East London, although Saltley would only have Class 08s on site that were Tinsley-allocated, but outbased in the Midlands.

No. 50007, 20 February 1994

No. 50007 (D407) *Sir Edward Elgar* is seen stabled along with classmate No. 50033 *Glorious*. This was at the end of their British Rail careers, as they were only used on railtours and they were withdrawn the following month. They had worked the previous day's Class 50 Western Memorial Tour from Crewe to Gloucester via London Paddington and Exeter.

No. 60066, 20 February 1994

No. 60066 *John Logie Baird* is seen having left the depot carrying Trainload Coal livery. This shot was taken opposite the power signal box, next to the staff bicycle racks. John Logie Baird was the inventor of the television.

No. 37057, 17 April 1994

No. 37057 (D6757) is seen moving round the yard carrying large logo livery, complete with unofficial Tinsley name *Viking*. By this time, this livery was becoming scarce on the Class 37 fleet, with most being repainted into Trainload liveries or departmental grey. No. 37057 is still in use today, working for Colas Rail Freight.

No. 47367, 24 April 1994

No. 47367 (D1886) is seen carrying red stripe Railfreight livery and the name *Kenny Cockbird*; the loco is also complete with a Stratford Cockney Sparrow depot sticker. It would be transferred to Freightliner use. No. 47367 is today based on the Mid-Norfolk Railway.

No. 47492, 24 April 1994

No. 47492 (D1760) is seen looking scruffy, carrying InterCity ScotRail livery. The yellow crane in the background was one of two that were used in the Landor Street Freightliner terminal, although both have now been replaced with newer cranes. Despite the livery, No. 47492 was a Crewe-based parcels locomotive at the time.

No. 47588, 29 May 1994

No. 47588 (D1773, Nos 47178, 47737) *Resurgent* is seen carrying the then new Rail Express Systems livery. RES inherited a motley collection of Class 47 locomotives and started a refurbishment programme, with the locos becoming Class 47/7s in the process. No. 47588 would be renumbered 47737.

No. 47471, 6 June 1994

No. 47471 (D1598) is seen still carrying original InterCity livery, complete with *Norman Tunna G.C.* nameplates. This was another Class 47 used by the parcels sector, and it would be withdrawn still carrying this livery. It would be scrapped by Ron Hull Junior, Rotherham, in 2005.

No. 31268, 19 June 1994

No. 31268 (D5698) is seen stabled carrying Civil Engineers 'Dutch' livery. By this time, the siding outside the office block had been shortened, as it used to extend round and finish next to the building with the water tank on top of it.

No. 47231, 26 December 1994

No. 47231 (D1907, No. 57010) is seen spending Christmas 1994 stabled on the depot. No. 47231 carries a very scruffy version of Trainload Speedlink livery, and the scar on the bodyside is where it has lost the name *The Silcock Express*. There was still some of its original two-tone green paint on the bodyside underneath the nameplate. No. 47231 was later rebuilt as No. 57010.

No. 47323, 26 December 1994

No. 47323 (D1804) is seen carrying Railfreight Distribution livery and also the name *Rover Group Quality Assured*. This loco carried this name due to the large amount of traffic generated by the Rover plant at Longbridge, for which Saltley was responsible for the haulage. The factory has since closed and has been demolished.

No. 47805, 26 December 1994

No. 47805 (D1935, Nos 47257, 47650) spends Christmas 1994 stabled round the back of the fuel shed. The InterCity Class 47s were still going strong at this time, with their replacements not due for another eight years. No. 47805 carries the name *Bristol Bath Road*.

No. 47827, 26 December 1994

No. 47827 (D1928, Nos 47251, 47589, 57302) is seen on the fuel pumps inside the fuel shed along with another InterCity-liveried classmate. No. 47827 would be rebuilt as No. 57302 for Virgin Trains.

No. 47828, 26 December 1994

No. 47828 (D1966, Nos 47266, 47629) is seen stabled on the line that goes round the back of the fuel shed. The line immediately behind No. 47828, which is a bit overgrown, leads into the Dunn Brothers scrapyard and is still in situ today.

No. 47831, 25 March 1995

No. 47831 (D1618, Nos 47037, 47563, 57310) poses in the sun outside the office block on a spring morning. No. 47831 was named *Bolton Wanderer*, and would be rebuilt as No. 57310 for Virgin Trains. The Class 47s were used on services to Manchester, Plymouth and Reading, and also to Bournemouth and Brighton at this time, until their eventual replacement by Class 220/221 Voyager units.

No. 47773, 10 September 1995

No. 47773 (D1755, No. 47541) is seen carrying RES livery, and also the name *Reservist*. This loco was more famous in its previous guise of No. 47541 *The Queen Mother*. No. 47773 is still in use today, based at Tyseley and working for Vintage Trains.

No. 47219, 26 December 1995

No. 47219 (D1869) *Arnold Kunzler* is seen on the fuel pumps alongside classmate No. 47826. By this time a lot of the work and staff had gone out from Saltley, with most of the passenger side transferring to New Street, leaving just Railfreight Distribution using the depot for staff. Arnold Kunzler was the founder of the MAT Group.

No. 47370, 26 December 1995

No. 47370 (D1889) is seen waiting its turn for the fuel pumps. This loco carries Railfreight Distribution livery, but it would soon lose its markings as it would transfer to Freightliner. Note the 'Welcome to Saltley' sign, a nice touch for visiting train crew.

No. 47349, 14 April 1996

No. 47349 (D1830, No. 57603) is seen carrying unbranded Trainload Railfreight livery. Of note is the Continental covered steel carrying wagon, a most unusual visitor to the depot. At this time, the depot had received a good clean up, resulting in a much improved appearance. No. 47349 was eventually rebuilt as No. 57603 for Great Western sleeper services.

No. 47236, 9 March 1997

No. 47236 (D1913) is seen stabled, carrying Railfreight Distribution livery. RFD were responsible for the automotive traffic generated by the Rover plant at Longbridge, with Class 47s operating in multiple, with the connection sockets situated in the former headcode box. No. 47236 was the second Class 47 to carry the name *Rover Group Quality Assured* after the original owner, No. 47323, was transferred to Freightliner.

No. 60065, 11 March 1997

No. 60065 *Kinder Low* is seen carrying Transrail markings, covering over its former Trainload Petroleum decals. Sectorisation, leading to privatization, was well underway by this time, with Saltley being an RFD depot.

No. 09011, 28 April 1997

No. 09011 (D4099) is seen stabled after privatization had been implemented on British Railways. No. 09011 was named unofficially as *Sudbury* and was allocated to Tinsley, Sheffield, but outbased at Saltley. Although the writing was not quite on the wall for Saltley at this time, the future was definitely not rosy.

No. 47339, 14 May 1997

No. 47339 (D1820) is seen stabled, carrying Freightliner grey livery. Freightliner Class 47s visited the depot, but not in vast numbers, as the depot was home to the outbased Tinsley fleet of RFD Class 47s. No. 47339 would be scrapped by Booth Roe Metals, Rotherham, in 2005.

No. 60041, 15 May 1997

No. 60041 is seen having emerged from the fuel shed, carrying EWS maroon livery. EWS took over most of the freight operation, excluding Freightliner, in 1996, having already added RES to its operations. It later acquired Railfreight Distribution as well, including Saltley depot.

No. 60081, 22 May 1997

No. 60081 is seen with Transrail logos covering over its former Trainload Metals decals. By now Saltley had become an EWS depot and, along with Bescot near Walsall, became one of the main hubs for the company in the West Midlands. Note the old two-axle tank wagon next to the Class 47 on the left; this used to be situated at the end of the headshunt behind the photographer.

No. 60017, 27 June 1997

No. 60017 *Shotton Works Centenary Year 1996* is seen stabled along with Nos 47287 and 37211. All three locos were operated by EWS at the time, despite the different liveries. The commencement of Class 66 deliveries on the horizon was a death knell for many older locomotives.

No. 47976, 19 October 1997

No. 47976 (D1747, No. 47546) stands wearing Civil Engineers 'Dutch' livery. This was named *Aviemore Centre* at the time, and was allocated to Bescot. The Civil Engineers fleet also passed to EWS, and they were used on ballast work.

No. 66031, 27 December 1998

No. 66031 is seen on crew training duty outside the main depot buildings. This loco had only been in the country for less than a month, and the rate at which the Class 66s were delivered was phenomenal, resulting in many older locomotives being condemned quickly.

No. 66044, 1 January 1999

No. 66044 is seen here also on crew training duty. This had arrived in the UK on 17 December, just two weeks previously, and the class was delivered at around a dozen examples per month.

No. 66065, 22 March 1999

No. 66065 is seen, showing the demise of many older classes of locomotives as there are only Class 66s in the shot. The Class 66s would not only lead to a withdrawal of locomotives, but they would also be another nail in Saltley's coffin.

No. 66104, 23 May 1999

No. 66104 is seen less than a month after landing in the UK. The Class 66s took over most jobs from the older locomotives. This was a further blow to Saltley, as not as many locomotives were needed, and the EWS fleet started to shrink in number.

No. 47709, 24 May 1999

No. 47709 (D1942, No. 47499) is seen carrying Fragonset livery. These locomotives were often hired out to Virgin Trains to cover for their own Class 47 unavailability. No. 47709 was scrapped by DRS at Eastleigh Works in 2012.

No. 47760, 29 July 1999

No. 47760 (D1617, Nos 47036, 47562, 47672) *Ribblehead Viaduct* is seen at a busy Saltley carrying EWS livery. Despite the influx of newer Class 66 locomotives, there were a few older locos that received EWS livery.

D9000, 22 October 1999

D9000 (No. 55022) *Royal Scots Grey* is seen on the stabling lines, carrying original green livery. This had been based at Saltley during the summer months, as it was used by Virgin Trains on its Saturday-only Birmingham New Street to Ramsgate service.

No. 08884, 30 April 2000

No. 08884 (D4098) is seen stabled while still carrying BR blue livery and its double arrow. It has been unofficially named *Saltley Seagulls*, after its famous train crew.

No. 47848, 30 April 2000

No. 47848 (D1652, Nos 47068, 47632) is seen carrying recently applied Virgin Trains livery. VT operated Cross Country at this time, and still retained a fleet of Class 47 locos; however, they would only survive until 2002, when they were replaced by Class 220/221 Voyager units. This was another blow to Saltley, as the Class 47s would no longer visit for fuel.

No. 66084, 24 August 2000

No. 66084 is seen stabled, awaiting its next turn of duty. As can be seen, deliveries of diesel fuel had changed from rail delivered to road delivered by this time, with the fuel truck in the background.

No. 92031, 6 June 2001

No. 92031 is seen making a most unusual visit to the depot, prior to its naming the following week. It was named *The Institute of Logistics and Transport*. This was one of only two Class 92s to carry full EWS livery.

No. 66224, 14 August 2001

No. 66224 is seen stabled along with other classmates. By this time the future of the depot was in doubt, as the main Rover traffic out of Longbridge was dwindling and the yard at Washwood Heath was modernized, including the addition of a refueling facility.

No. 47798, 7 November 2001

No. 47798 (D1656, Nos 47072, 47609, 47834) *Prince William* is seen stabled carrying Royal Train livery. In the background stored Nos 08939 and 47634 can be seen. By this time the number of locos visiting the depot was decreasing. No. 47798 would become part of the National Collection, based at York.

No. 60100, 7 January 2002

No. 60100 is seen with Mainline branding covering over its former Trainload Construction decals. No. 60100 carries the name *Boar of Badenoch*, and is still in use with DB Cargo today.

No. 60038, 8 April 2002

No. 60038 *AvestaPolarit* is seen having been freshly repainted into EWS livery. No. 47634 behind is showing signs of being stripped for spares; it would never work again.

No. 47787, 2 May 2002

No. 47787 (D1757, Nos 47163, 47610, 47823) *Windsor Castle* is seen having been spruced up for Royal Train duty. This was the back-up for normal Royal Train locos Nos 47798 and 47799. No. 47787 is still in use today with West Coast Trains, although it is currently stored at Carnforth.

No. 158815, 13 May 2002

No. 158815 is seen stabled on the depot, carrying Alphaline Wales and Borders branding. These units were stabled on Saltley for a short while during this time. No. 158815 is still in use today with Northern.

No. 86426, 9 June 2002

No. 86426 (E3195, Nos 86026, 86326) *Pride of the Nation* is seen stabled at Saltley, awaiting onward transfer to Toton. It was visiting Toton for a repaint into Freightliner green livery, as it was about to be hired to them.

No. 47734, 26 August 2002

No. 47734 (D1767, Nos 47172, 47583) is seen stabled along with classmate No. 47757. EWS would lose the Royal Mail contract the following year, making these locomotives redundant – another blow to Saltley. No. 47734 carries the name *Crewe Diesel Depot Quality Approved*.

No. 66103, 8 May 2003

No. 66103 is seen during the depot's final couple of years in use. The locomotive inspection point would close two years later, in 2005.

No. 47830, 23 July 2003

No. 47830 (D1645, Nos 47061, 47649) carries plain Great Western green livery, and the depot is now starting to become overgrown and unkempt. No. 47830 is still in use today, working for Freightliner, and carries original two-tone green livery.

No. 56078, 1 April 2004

No. 56078 *Doncaster Enterprise* is seen stored on the depot. The loco had worked the previous day's Twilight Grids Railtour along with No. 56115, which was also on the depot, and they had brought the curtain down on the EWS Class 56 operation.

No. 47791, 2 October 2005

No. 47791 (D1969, Nos 47268, 47595, 47675) is seen withdrawn on the line near the office block. This was the very last locomotive to leave the depot, but it didn't leave until 2008, three years after the depot had closed to locomotives, thus bringing to an end a once very famous depot.